D0463095

Blender

Blender

Perfect sauces, soups, purées, and smoothies

Linda Doeser

p

This is a Parragon Publishing Book
First published in 2005

Parragon Publishing
Queen Street House
4 Queen Street
Bath
BA1 1HE, UK

ISBN: 1-40545-117-3

Printed in China

Author: Linda Doeser
Editor: Fiona Biggs
Designed by Fiona Roberts
Photography: Karen Thomas
Home Economist: Annie Nichols

Notes for the Reader

This book uses both imperial and US cup measurements. All spoon measurements are
level; teaspoons are assumed to be 5 ml and tablespoons are assumed to be 15 ml.
Unless otherwise stated, milk is assumed to be full fat, individual vegetables such as
potatoes are medium, and pepper is freshly ground black pepper. Recipes using raw or
very lightly cooked eggs should be avoided by infants, the elderly, pregnant women,
convalescents and anyone suffering from an illness. Pregnant and breastfeeding women
are advised to avoid eating peanuts and peanut products. The times given are an
approximate guide only. Preparation times differ according to the techniques used by
different people and the cooking times may also vary from those given. Optional
ingredients, variations, or serving suggestions have not been included in the calculations.

Contents

INTRODUCTION

A blender is not only one of the most useful appliances to have in the kitchen but also one of the most common. Yet, strangely, it is often under-used. Most people have their own standard recipes for which they invariably get the blender out of storage.

A mom with a young baby might use it for puréeing tiny portions of family dishes, a keen gardener might make batches of soup for the freezer when there is a glut of vegetables, and an enthusiastic hostess might press it into service for dips, pâtés, and terrines. Yet the rest of the time, it is frequently overlooked and unused.

This is a shame as the blender really is the cook's friend and can take care of all sorts of tedious and time-consuming tasks effortlessly and quickly. It's rather like having your very own assistant chef. For example, think how often recipes call for bread crumbs, whether for homemade burgers or stuffing for the Thanksgiving turkey. Why make your arm ache and risk grazing your fingers on a grater, when you can produce them quickly and painlessly in the blender? Recipes frequently specify chopped or even finely chopped herbs. Save time and effort by doing this in the blender. It's also great for making smoothies and milkshakes, fruit drinks, and wonderfully frothy hot chocolate.

In the recipes in this book the blender plays a more central role, although, of course, it can still be used for the initial preparation of ingredients, such as chopping nuts. The recipes amply demonstrate what a labor-saving device

this clever appliance is and will, it is hoped, inspire you to new culinary heights. Take something as simple and popular as mayonnaise, for example. Of course, there are many commercial varieties available but these often contain flavorings and other additives and tend to be unappetizingly gelatinous in texture. Moreover, "real" mayonnaise tastes so much better. However, it is an incredible bore to make by hand and the temptation to try to speed up the process, in spite of the fact that this results in curdled egg yolk, is almost irresistible. Making it in the blender will spare your aching wrist and also allows you to achieve the precise consistency that suits you. As a bonus, the basic recipe (see page 28) also includes two other mayonnaise-based sauces.

Types of blender

There are basically two types of blender—goblet and hand-held. The recipes in this book are designed for a goblet blender, sometimes also known as a liquidizer.

Goblet blender: This consists of a base in which the motor is located and a removable tall cylindrical bowl, or goblet, with a lid. It may be a single, free-standing appliance or part of a combination with a food processor or electric mixer. The goblet is usually made of transparent plastic or glass and varies in capacity from about 2½ cups to 6½ cups. Many have a handle and a pouring lip and they usually have a hole in the lid through which ingredients can be added while the motor is running—this is essential for some recipes, such as Hollandaise Sauce (see page 38). A graduated scale on the side of the goblet makes measuring liquids very simple and most blender goblets also have a line designating the maximum capacity that the blender can safely cope with at any one time.

There are four small, extremely sharp blades located in the base of the goblet at right angles to each other. As these rotate the center of the mixture forms a well and the mixture is pushed up the sides of the goblet and then falls back down onto the blades. Unlike in food processors, the blades are not usually removable.

The blender, once plugged in, is operated by an on/off switch and may also have a switch or dial that allows you to vary the speed. Some models also have a pulse mode. As most blending needs to take place at high speed, a single-speed appliance should not present much problem. Lower speeds are generally used only for chopping. The blender will continue to run until you switch it off, although the manufacturer usually includes a safety cut-out. Nowadays, blenders are made so that they will not switch on until the lid is properly fitted. When they were first introduced in the 1950s, this was not always the case and people sometimes had unfortunate accidents when the contents of the blender were sprayed all over the kitchen or, far worse, they were badly injured by foolishly inserting their fingers while the motor was still running.

Hand-held blender: This has a handle and a wand at the base of which is a rotating blade. The motor is located in the handle which also incorporates the switch. It has a single speed and works for as long as the control switch, also on the handle, is depressed or in the on position. This is an in-built safety feature. Some models have extra attachments, such as a whisk, and interchangeable blades. This type of blender is useful for blending small quantities, particularly when they are still in a pan. It cannot be used for all the recipes in this book, but works well for some sauces, soups, and drinks, for example. It is not usually suitable for blending dry ingredients.

Choosing a blender

The cost of blenders can vary considerably, so if you're not going to be using one frequently, it is sensible to avoid the more expensive and sophisticated models. If you are a very enthusiastic cook a combined blender and mixer or blender and food processor might be the best choice, but remember that this will take up a lot of space. The size of your family is also a consideration. If you will be preparing only small quantities, a large goblet is more trouble than it's worth as the food tends to get lost inside it. A mom with a baby might find a medium-size goblet blender is ideal for adult foods, while an inexpensive hand-held blender is more appropriate for preparing infant purées.

Using a goblet blender

As with all electrical appliances, it is important to read the manufacturer's instructions. These will always include information about safe running times and maximum capacity, as well as advice about the kinds of foods that are suitable for processing in a blender, and the care and maintenance of your particular model.

Make sure that the blender is standing securely on a flat surface and that the electrical cord is not overhanging. Fit the goblet into position. Blenders work best with relatively small quantities of ingredients, so it is often better to process in two or more batches. This is particularly important if you are using the blender to chop dry ingredients, such as vegetables. Never fill the blender with more than the specified maximum capacity and, in the case of liquid, which is inclined to froth up, it should not be more than one-third to one-half full. Never leave the blender switched on and unattended and make sure that it is out of the reach of children.

Batters: Blend the egg, milk and any other liquids to combine them, then, with the motor running, gradually add the dry ingredients through the hole in the lid.

Chopping: Cut vegetables, fruit, cheese, chocolate, chicken, etc. into fairly small pieces of about the same size. Remove pits and bones and process in small batches at maximum speed. Tip the first batch into a bowl before adding the next. If you are chopping candied peel, cut it into fairly small pieces, then process in small batches with a little sugar to prevent it from sticking.

Cooked foods and leftovers: These are best processed with the addition of a little stock, water, gravy, fruit juice, wine, or other liquid that is appropriate to the flavor. Cut large pieces into smaller, even-sized pieces before adding them to the blender and process in small batches. If you are processing stews, casseroles, and soups, make sure that you include liquid with the solid ingredients.

Bread crumbs: Tear slices of bread into small pieces and break up cookies. With the motor running, drop these into the blender through the hole in the lid. Process in small batches. For dry bread crumbs, use day-old bread and dry it in a preheated oven, 250°F, for 20–25 minutes before breaking it into pieces and processing in the blender.

Nuts: These should be processed in small batches at low speed. Turn the blender on and off during processing for maximum fineness.

Herbs: Strip the leaves from the stems and, with the motor running, drop them into the blender through the hole in the lid. They can be coarsely or finely chopped.

Ice cubes: Blenders are not usually robust enough to cope with whole ice cubes. Use cracked ice when making slushes and other drinks (see page 73).

Purées: When making terrines, pâtés, and infant foods, chop the ingredients into fairly small pieces before processing in small batches. Dips can usually be processed in larger quantities. When processing cooked vegetables and fruit, such as boiled carrots and stewed apples, and raw soft vegetables and fruit, such as avocados and raspberries, fill the goblet no more than one-third full. Extra liquid is not required. Process on high speed and scrape down the sides occasionally. To get rid of seeds, press the purée through a fine nylon strainer.

Soups: Let cool slightly before pouring into the blender. Err on the side of caution and do not fill more than half full. Hold the lid firmly before switching on.

Note: Do not grind coffee beans or spices in a blender.

Using a hand-held blender

This is a convenient way to purée small quantities of food and to blend sauces and soups in the pan. Read the manufacturer's instructions for guidance on your model. Many are not suitable for chopping dry ingredients, for example. Put the wand into the pan or bowl—don't immerse the handle—and switch on, then move the wand smoothly through the ingredients in a figure eight. Small quantities of splashy ingredients, such as batters, are best blended in a pitcher. A hand-held blender can be used for processing creamy dips, most soups, eggs for omelets and scrambled egg, many sauces, soft fruits, and butter frosting. It is also suitable for beating ice cream and sherbets during freezing and for preparing cheesecake fillings.

Hints and tips

◎ When chopping ingredients in the blender, process in small batches. If there is too much in the blender, part will be finely chopped, while the rest will be in larger pieces.

◎ To avoid ingredients sticking, make sure there is sufficient liquid and that the blender is not too full. When processing thick mixtures scrape down the sides of the goblet with a spatula from time to time.

◎ Always use plastic utensils when scraping down the sides of the goblet and spooning a mixture out of it to avoid scratching the sides. For the same reason, don't clean the goblet with scouring pads or abrasives.

◎ If liquid leaks out of the top of the blender, switch off, mop up and remove some of the liquid. Soups and drinks tend to froth up, so never more than half-fill the goblet.

◎ Lumpy sauces, soups, and purées need longer processing. If you're worried about the motor overheating, stop and let it cool for a few minutes before continuing.

◎ Keep an eye on what you're doing to avoid over-processing. If you are chopping dried fruit in a blender without paying attention, you'll end up with a purée.

◎ If the motor cuts out during use, switch off, wait for 15–20 minutes for the motor to cool, then try again. If the blender still won't work, check the fuse.

Care of the blender

Switch off and unplug the blender before washing it. Check the manufacturer's instructions for dishwasher safety. Otherwise, wash the goblet in warm, soapy water. Rinse and dry thoroughly. Remember that the blades are very sharp. Stubborn stains can usually be removed with a little vegetable oil. If food is trapped in the blades, pour a little soapy water into the goblet, fit it back in the base unit, and switch on briefly. Rinse and dry thoroughly. Never immerse the base in water. Simply wipe with a damp cloth and then dry. Switch off a hand-held blender and remove the wand. Wash in warm, soapy water, rinse, and dry. If the wand is not detachable, wash the blades with warm soapy water without getting the handle wet. Rinse and dry.

CHAPTER 1: SOUPS

GAZPACHO

This is probably the world's best-known chilled soup. It's so tasty and colorful it certainly deserves its reputation.

Serves 6

Preparation time: 30 minutes, plus 2 hours' chilling

Cooking time: 2–3 minutes

Ingredients

9 oz white bread slices, crusts removed

1 lb 9 oz tomatoes, peeled and chopped

3 garlic cloves, coarsely chopped

2 red bell peppers, seeded and chopped

1 cucumber, peeled, seeded, and chopped

5 tbsp extra virgin olive oil

5 tbsp red wine vinegar

1 tbsp tomato paste

3¾ pints water

salt and pepper

To garnish

2 tbsp olive oil

1 garlic clove, finely chopped

4 slices white bread, crusts removed and
  cut into ¼-inch cubes

6 scallions, thinly sliced

¼ cucumber, diced

1 Tear the bread into pieces and place in the blender. Process briefly to make bread crumbs and transfer to a large bowl. Add the tomatoes, garlic, bell peppers, cucumber, olive oil, vinegar, and tomato paste. Mix well

2 Working in batches, place the tomato mixture with about the same amount of the measured water in the blender and process to a purée. Transfer to another bowl. When all the tomato mixture and water have been blended together, stir well and season to taste with salt and pepper. Cover with plastic wrap and chill in the refrigerator for at least 2 hours, but no longer than 12 hours.

3 Heat the oil in a heavy skillet. Add the garlic and the bread cubes and cook over medium heat, stirring and tossing frequently, for 2–3 minutes until golden brown. Remove from the skillet with a slotted spoon and drain on paper towels.

4 Arrange the garnishes on separate small dishes and serve with the soup.

Cook's tip
Other traditional garnishes for gazpacho include seeded and finely diced red and green bell peppers and chopped hard-cooked egg.

CHILLED AVOCADO SOUP

This delicate soup is made entirely in the blender and is perfect for an al fresco meal. Serve within 2 hours of making to avoid discoloration.

🍽️ Serves 4

🥣 Preparation time: 10 minutes, plus 30 minutes' chilling

🧤 Cooking time: 0 minutes

Ingredients

1 tbsp lemon juice

2 avocados

1 tbsp snipped fresh chives, plus extra to garnish

1 tbsp chopped fresh flat-leaf parsley

scant 2 cups cold chicken stock

1 1/4 cups light cream, plus
  extra to garnish

dash of Worcestershire sauce

salt and pepper

1 Put the lemon juice into the blender. Halve the avocados and remove the pits. Scoop out the flesh and chop coarsely.

2 Place the avocado flesh, chives, parsley, stock, cream, and Worcestershire sauce in the blender and process to a smooth purée.

3 Transfer to a bowl and season to taste with salt and pepper. Cover the bowl tightly with plastic wrap and chill in the refrigerator for at least 30 minutes. To serve, stir, then ladle into chilled soup bowls, and garnish with a swirl of cream and a sprinkling of snipped chives.

Cook's tip

Avocado flesh turns an unappealing brownish color when exposed to the air. It is important to put the lemon juice into the blender before you add the avocado to help prevent this. It is also important that the soup is tightly covered while chilling.

Variation

For a vegetarian version of this soup, substitute vegetable stock for the chicken stock. If you like, you can use plain yogurt instead of light cream.

TOMATO SOUP

Once you have tasted homemade tomato soup you'll never want to buy the canned version again.

 Serves 4

Preparation time: 15 minutes

Cooking time: 25 minutes

Ingredients

¼ cup butter

1 small onion, finely chopped

1 lb tomatoes, coarsely chopped

1 bay leaf

3 tbsp all-purpose flour

2½ cups milk

salt and pepper

2 tbsp torn fresh basil leaves, to garnish

1 Melt half the butter in a pan. Add the onion and cook over low heat, stirring occasionally, for 5–6 minutes until softened. Add the tomatoes and bay leaf and cook, stirring occasionally, for 15 minutes, or until pulpy.

2 Meanwhile, melt the remaining butter in another pan. Add the flour and cook, stirring constantly, for 1 minute. Remove the pan from the heat and gradually stir in the milk. Return to the heat, season with salt and pepper, and bring to a boil, stirring constantly. Continue to cook, stirring, until smooth and thickened. Transfer to the top of a double boiler.

3 When the tomatoes are pulpy, remove the pan from the heat. Discard the bay leaf and pour the tomato mixture into the blender. Process until smooth, then push through a fine strainer into a clean pan. Bring the tomato purée to the boil, then gradually stir it into the milk mixture. Season to taste with salt and pepper. Ladle into warm bowls, garnish with basil leaves, and serve immediately.

Cook's tip

It is essential that the tomatoes are really ripe for maximum flavor and sweetness. Ideally, use homegrown, sun-ripened tomatoes or vine tomatoes. If these are not available, you may need to add 1–2 teaspoons sugar to sweeten the purée.

Variation

Add ½ cup diced lean bacon with the onion in step 1 and garnish the soup with 2 tablespoons chopped fresh parsley instead of basil.

CREAMY CARROT SOUP

With its attractive color and sweet, rich flavor, this easy soup is always popular with all the family.

⦿ Serves 4

Preparation time: 20 minutes

Cooking time: 25 minutes

Ingredients

¼ cup butter

1 onion, finely chopped

1 leek, finely chopped

3 ¼ cups grated carrots

1 tbsp all-purpose flour

5 cups hot chicken or
  vegetable stock

⅔ cup heavy cream

salt and pepper

fresh basil leaves, to garnish (optional)

1 Melt the butter in a large, heavy pan. Add the onion and leek and cook, stirring occasionally, for 5–6 minutes until softened. Stir in the carrots, lower the heat, cover, and cook for 5 minutes.

2 Sprinkle in the flour and cook, stirring, for 1 minute. Gradually stir in the hot stock. Bring to a boil, then simmer for 8 minutes.

3 Remove the pan from the heat and let the soup cool slightly. Pour it into the blender and process to a purée. Transfer to a clean pan and bring back to a simmer. Stir in the cream and simmer for 2 minutes more. Season to taste, ladle into warm bowls, and serve, garnished with basil leaves, if desired.

Cook's tip
You can use the blender to chop the onion, leek, and carrots into small dice. Chop them coarsely first, then process in small batches at maximum speed.

THAI PORK & SHRIMP SOUP

Soup is almost always served as part of a Thai meal and is often eaten as a snack, so recipes are many, varied, and utterly delicious.

Serves 6
Preparation time: 20 minutes
Cooking time: 1 hour 10 minutes

Ingredients

6 oz pork tenderloin, cut into very thin strips

scant ½ cup Thai jasmine rice

6¼ cups chicken stock

scant 2 cups coconut milk

3 tbsp lime juice

1 tbsp Thai fish sauce

2 garlic cloves, chopped

1 lemongrass stalk, finely chopped

2 kaffir lime leaves

1 fresh green chili, seeded and chopped

2 tbsp chopped fresh cilantro

2⅔ cups cooked, peeled shrimp

fresh cilantro sprigs, sliced into julienne strips,
   to garnish

1 Put the pork, rice, stock, coconut milk, lime juice, fish sauce, garlic, lemongrass, kaffir lime leaves, chili, and half the cilantro into a large pan and bring to a boil over medium heat. Lower the heat, cover, and simmer, stirring occasionally, for 1 hour.

2 Remove from the heat and let cool slightly. Remove and discard the kaffir lime leaves, then transfer to the blender, and process to a smooth purée.

3 Transfer the soup to a clean pan and bring to a boil. Add the shrimp and cook for 2–3 minutes more until heated through. Ladle into warm bowls, garnish with the cilantro strips, and serve.

Cook's tip
Thai jasmine rice, sometimes called fragrant rice, Thai fish sauce, canned coconut milk, lemongrass, and kaffir lime leaves are available from most supermarkets and specialty Asian food stores.

Variation
For a more substantial soup, add 8 oz drained canned straw mushrooms with the shrimp in step 3. Alternatively, substitute 1 lb peeled raw jumbo shrimp for the cooked shrimp. Add them in step 3 and simmer for 5 minutes, or until they turn pink.

SHRIMP BISQUE

*A bisque is a thick, creamy fish soup based on a shellfish purée
and has a long and venerable history.*

 Serves 4

Preparation time: 30 minutes

Cooking time: 45–50 minutes

Ingredients

1 lb raw shrimp	4 tbsp fresh white bread crumbs
1 tbsp sunflower oil	3 tbsp butter
2 shallots, sliced	pinch of freshly grated nutmeg
1 celery stalk, sliced (reserve leaves for garnish)	$^2/_3$ cup dry white wine
1 carrot, sliced	1 large egg yolk
2 tsp lemon juice	$^2/_3$ cup heavy cream
1 tbsp tomato paste	salt and pepper

1 Pull off the heads and peel the shrimp, reserving the heads and shells. Place the shrimp in a dish, cover with plastic wrap, and store in the refrigerator until required.

2 Heat the oil in a large pan. Add the shrimp heads and shells and cook over high heat, stirring frequently, for 3–5 minutes. Lower the heat, add the shallots, celery, and carrot, and cook, stirring occasionally, for 5–6 minutes. Pour in 5 cups water and add 1 teaspoon of the lemon juice and the tomato paste. Bring to a boil, lower the heat, cover, and simmer for 25 minutes.

3 Remove the stock from the heat and strain into a bowl. Discard the contents of the strainer. Place the bread crumbs in another bowl and add scant 2 cups of the stock while it is still hot, then set aside.

4 Melt 2 tablespoons of the butter in a pan and add the shrimp. Cook, stirring and tossing constantly for 5 minutes. Add the nutmeg, remaining lemon juice, and the bread crumb and stock mixture and cook gently, stirring occasionally, for 5 minutes more. Beat in the remaining butter.

5 Remove the mixture from the heat and transfer to the blender. Process to a smooth purée, transfer to a clean pan. and set over medium heat. Add the wine and remaining stock and bring to a boil.

6 Remove the pan from the heat and season with salt and pepper. Combine the egg yolk and cream in a small bowl, then stir the mixture into the soup. Return to very low heat and cook for 1–2 minutes, but do not let the soup boil. Serve immediately, garnished with celery leaves.

CHICKEN SOUP

This creamy soup is the ultimate in comfort food, although

it is also special enough to serve to guests.

Serves 6

Preparation time: 20 minutes, plus cooling

Cooking time: 1 ¼ hours

Ingredients

3 lb chicken

1 bunch of fresh parsley

1 bay leaf

½ tsp freshly grated nutmeg

1 tbsp butter

2 tbsp all-purpose flour

3 tbsp heavy cream

salt and pepper

1 Place the chicken in a large pan, add the parsley, bay leaf, and nutmeg, and season well with salt. Pour in 6¼ cups water and bring to a boil, skimming off any scum that rises to the surface. Lower the heat, cover, and simmer gently for 1 hour.

2 Remove the pan from the heat and transfer the chicken to a cutting board. Strain the stock into a bowl and let cool. Remove and discard the skin and bones from the chicken. Cut the flesh into small pieces.

3 Skim the fat from the top of the cooled stock, then place the stock and chicken in the blender. Process to a smooth purée. You may need to do this in batches. Transfer the soup to a clean pan.

4 Make a beurre manié by blending together the butter and flour with a fork until a smooth paste forms. Bring the soup just to boiling point, then whisk in the beurre manié in small pieces at a time. Bring to a boil, stirring constantly, then lower the heat, and simmer for 10 minutes. Stir in the cream and season to taste with salt and pepper. Ladle into warm bowls, sprinkle with freshly ground black pepper, and serve immediately.

Cook's tip

To speed up the cooling process, place the bowl containing the stock in another bowl of ice cubes or in a sink of very cold water. It is easiest to remove the fat once it has congealed on the surface.

Variation

For an even more flavorful soup, substitute chicken or vegetable stock for the water in step 1.

CHAPTER 2: SAUCES

MAYONNAISE

This wonderfully versatile sauce is used for salad dressings and sandwich fillings and many different extra flavorings can be added.

Serves 4
Preparation time: 5 minutes
Cooking time: 0 minutes

Ingredients

Basic Mayonnaise

2 extra large egg yolks

1 tbsp lemon juice or white
   wine vinegar

1/4 tsp mustard powder

2/3 cup sunflower oil

2/3 cup extra virgin
   olive oil

salt and pepper

Rémoulade Sauce

2 eggs, hard-cooked, cooled,
   and shelled

1 egg yolk

1 tbsp lemon juice or white
   wine vinegar

1 1/2 tsp Dijon mustard

2/3 cup sunflower oil

2/3 cup extra virgin
   olive oil

2 tbsp chopped, mixed, fresh
   parsley, chives, and chervil

2 dill pickles, drained and very
   finely chopped

1 tbsp bottled capers, drained

salt and pepper

Garlic Mayonnaise

2 extra large egg yolks

1 tbsp lemon juice or white
   wine vinegar

5–6 garlic cloves, crushed

2/3 cup sunflower oil

2/3 cup extra virgin
   olive oil

salt and pepper

1 To make **Basic Mayonnaise**, put the egg yolks, lemon juice, and mustard powder into the blender and season with a little salt and pepper. Process on medium speed for 5 seconds. With the motor running, gradually pour in both the oils through the opening in the lid. Continue processing for 1 minute, or until all the oil has been incorporated. If necessary, stop the blender and scrape down the sides with a spatula.

2 To make **Rémoulade Sauce**, rub the hard-cooked egg yolks through a fine strainer into the blender. (You won't need the whites.) Add the raw yolk and process briefly to mix. Add the lemon juice and mustard and season with a little salt and pepper. Process on medium speed for 5 seconds. With the motor running, gradually pour in both the oils through the opening in the lid. Continue processing for 1 minute, or until all the oil has been incorporated. Put the mayonnaise into a bowl and stir in the herbs, dill pickles, and capers. Serve with cold meat, fish and shellfish, and grated celery root.

3 To make **Garlic Mayonnaise**, put the egg yolks, lemon juice, and garlic into the blender and season with a little salt and pepper. Process on medium speed for 5 seconds. With the motor running, gradually pour in both the oils through the opening in the lid. Continue processing for 1 minute until all the oil has been incorporated.

ROUILLE

Traditionally served with bouillabaisse and other fish dishes, this spicy red bell pepper sauce is usually presented separately or spread on croutons.

Makes about ³/₄ cup
Preparation time: 15 minutes
Cooking time: 5–10 minutes

Ingredients

³/₄ cup fresh white bread crumbs

2 red bell peppers, halved and seeded

1 fresh red chili, seeded and coarsely chopped

3 garlic cloves, coarsely chopped

¹/₂ cup extra virgin olive oil

salt and pepper

1 Place the bread crumbs in a bowl and add water to cover, then set aside. Meanwhile, put the bell pepper halves, skin side up, on a cookie sheet and place under a preheated broiler. Cook for 5–10 minutes until the skins are blistered and charred. Remove the bell pepper halves with tongs, place in a plastic bag, and tie the top. Leave to cool.

2 When the bell peppers are cool enough to handle, peel off their skins, coarsely chop the flesh, and place in the blender. Squeeze the excess water from the bread crumbs and add to the blender with the chili and garlic. Season with salt and pepper.

3 Process to a smooth paste. With the motor running, gradually add the oil through the hole in the lid until it is fully incorporated. Stop and scrape down the sides of the blender as necessary. Transfer to a bowl, cover with plastic wrap, and store in the refrigerator until required.

Variation

For a lighter texture, omit the bread crumbs and add 1 egg yolk to the blender in step 2. You will probably need to add about 3 tablespoons extra olive oil in step 3. For saffron rouille, process 3 coarsely chopped garlic cloves, *1 seeded and chopped fresh red chili, 2 egg yolks, a large pinch of saffron threads, and some salt and pepper in the blender. Then, with the motor running, add 1 cup extra virgin olive oil through the hole in the lid.*

PESTO

Traditionally, pesto is made by hand, uses only basil, and is never served with anything other than pasta. These speedy versions, however, offer several choices.

◎ Makes about 1 cup

🥣 Preparation time: 5 minutes

🧤 Cooking time: 30–60 seconds (Sun-Dried Tomato Pesto)

Ingredients

Pesto Genovese	Sun-Dried Tomato Pesto	Tarragon Pesto
2 garlic cloves, coarsely chopped	$\frac{1}{4}$ cup pine nuts	2 garlic cloves, coarsely chopped
$\frac{1}{4}$ cup pine nuts	2 garlic cloves, coarsely chopped	$\frac{1}{4}$ cup blanched almonds, coarsely chopped
$\frac{3}{4}$ cup fresh basil leaves	8 oz sun-dried tomatoes in oil, drained and coarsely chopped	$\frac{3}{4}$ cup fresh tarragon leaves
1 tsp coarse salt	1 tsp coarse salt	1 tsp coarse salt
$\frac{1}{3}$ cup freshly grated Parmesan cheese	$\frac{1}{3}$ cup freshly grated Parmesan cheese	$\frac{1}{3}$ cup freshly grated Parmesan cheese
$\frac{1}{2}$–$\frac{2}{3}$ cup extra virgin olive oil	$\frac{1}{2}$–$\frac{2}{3}$ cup extra virgin olive oil	$\frac{1}{2}$–$\frac{2}{3}$ cup extra virgin olive oil

1 For the **Pesto Genovese**, put the garlic, pine nuts, basil leaves, and salt into the blender and process to a purée. Add the Parmesan and process briefly again. Then add $\frac{1}{2}$ cup of the oil and process again. If the consistency is too thick, add the remaining oil and process again until smooth.

2 For the **Sun-Dried Tomato Pesto**, dry-fry the pine nuts in a heavy skillet for 30–60 seconds until golden. Remove from the skillet and let cool, then place in the blender with the garlic, sun-dried tomatoes, and salt. Process to a purée. Add the Parmesan and process briefly again. Then add $\frac{1}{2}$ cup of the oil and process again. If the consistency is too thick, add the remaining oil and process again until smooth.

Cook's tip
Pesto can be used to liven up many dishes Simply coat pieces of fish and chicken or pork or lamb chops with the sauce, then bake or broil as you normally would.

Variation
You can ring the changes on the Basic Pesto Genovese with many different ingredients. Try substituting parsley for the basil and walnuts for the pine nuts or use half parsley and half arugula.

3 For the **Tarragon Pesto**, put the garlic, almonds, tarragon leaves, and salt into the blender and process to a purée. Add the Parmesan and process briefly again. Then add $1/2$ cup of the oil and process again. If the consistency is too thick, add the remaining oil and process again until smooth.

TAPENADE

This Provencal black olive paste is great simply stirred into freshly cooked pasta and is also delicious just served with toasted bread.

🍽 Makes about ¾ cup
🥣 Preparation time: 10 minutes
🧤 Cooking time: 0 minutes

Ingredients

3½ oz canned anchovy fillets

12 oz black olives, pitted and
   coarsely chopped

2 garlic cloves, coarsely chopped

2 tbsp capers, drained and rinsed

1 tbsp Dijon mustard

3 tbsp extra virgin olive oil

2 tbsp lemon juice

1 Drain the anchovies, reserving the oil from the can. Coarsely chop the fish and place in the blender. Add the reserved oil and all the remaining ingredients. Process to a smooth purée. Stop and scrape down the sides if necessary.

2 Transfer the tapenade to a dish, cover with plastic wrap, and chill in the refrigerator until required. If you are not planning to use the tapenade until the following day (or even the one after), cover the surface with a layer of olive oil to prevent it from drying out.

Cook's tip
This is quite a salty combination, so you may prefer to de-salt the anchovies first. Place them in a shallow dish, pour in enough cold water or milk to cover, and set aside for 5–10 minutes. Drain and proceed with the recipe.

Variation
For a more substantial version of tapenade, add 3½ oz drained canned tuna with the other ingredients. You may need to increase the quantity of oil. Add the extra oil in tablespoons at a time, blending after each addition until you achieve the required consistency.

WHITE SAUCES

Basic white sauce may be served completely plain or form the basis for an entire family of flavored sauces, some of which are listed here.

🍽 Makes 1 ¼ cups

🥣 Preparation time: 10 minutes, plus 20 minutes' standing (Béchamel Sauce)

🧤 Cooking time: 8–12 minutes

Ingredients

Basic White Sauce

2 tbsp butter, melted

¼ cup all-purpose flour

1 ¼ cups milk

salt and pepper

Béchamel Sauce

1 ¼ cups milk

1 slice onion

1 bay leaf

1 mace blade

5 black peppercorns

2 tbsp butter, melted

¼ cup all-purpose flour

salt and pepper

Cheese Sauce

2 tbsp butter, melted

¼ cup all purpose flour

1 ¼ cups milk

¾ cup grated Cheddar cheese,

cayenne pepper

salt and white pepper

Parsley Sauce

2 –3 fresh parsley sprigs

2 tbsp butter, melted

¼ cup all-purpose flour

1 ¼ cups milk

pinch of freshly grated nutmeg

salt and pepper

1 For the **Basic White Sauce**, put the butter, flour, and milk into the blender and process until smooth. Pour into a pan and bring to a boil over low heat, stirring constantly. Boil, stirring constantly, for 3–4 minutes until thickened and smooth. Remove from the heat and season to taste with salt and pepper.

2 For the **Béchamel Sauce**, pour the milk into a pan and add the onion, bay leaf, mace blade, and peppercorns. Heat gently to simmering point, then remove the pan from the heat, and set aside for 20 minutes to steep. Strain the milk into the blender, add the butter and flour, and process until smooth. Pour into a pan and bring to a boil over low heat, stirring constantly. Continue to boil, stirring constantly, for 3–4 minutes until thickened and smooth. Remove from the heat and season to taste with salt and pepper.

Cook's tip
To prevent a skin forming on the surface of a white sauce, place a sheet of dampened waxed paper on the sauce, directly on the surface so that the sauce sticks to it.

3 For the **Cheese Sauce**, put the butter, flour, and milk into the blender and process until smooth. Pour into a pan and bring to a boil over low heat, stirring constantly. Continue to boil, stirring constantly, for 3–4 minutes until thickened and smooth. Remove from the heat, stir in the grated cheese until melted, then season to taste with cayenne pepper, salt, and white pepper.

4 For the **Parsley Sauce**, blanch the parsley sprigs in a pan of boiling water for 30 seconds. Drain, refresh under cold water, then strip off the leaves, and chop finely. Put the butter, flour, and milk into the blender and process until smooth. Pour into a pan and bring to a boil over low heat, stirring constantly. Continue to boil, stirring constantly, for 3–4 minutes until thickened and smooth. Remove from the heat, stir in the parsley, and season to taste with nutmeg, salt, and pepper.

HOLLANDAISE SAUCE

A favorite with poached asparagus and essential for making eggs Benedict,
Hollandaise is also the basis for a family of sauces.

◎ Makes about ¾ cup

🥣 Preparation time: 10 minutes

🧤 Cooking time: 10 minutes (Béarnaise Sauce)

Ingredients

Basic Hollandaise Sauce	Béarnaise Sauce	Mousseline Sauce
3 egg yolks	5 tbsp white wine vinegar	3 egg yolks
1 tbsp lemon juice	2 shallots, finely chopped	1 tbsp lemon juice
1 tbsp warm water	1½ tbsp chopped	1 tbsp warm water
½ cup sweet butter, melted	fresh tarragon	½ cup sweet butter, melted
salt and pepper	1 fresh thyme sprig	salt and pepper
	½ bay leaf	½ cup heavy cream,
	3 egg yolks	stiffly whipped
	1 tbsp warm water	
	½ cup sweet butter, melted	
	salt and pepper	

1 For the **Basic Hollandaise Sauce**, put the egg yolks, lemon juice, and water into the blender and process on low speed very briefly to mix. With the motor running, gradually add the melted butter through the hole in the lid. Continue to process until the sauce is thickened. Do not over-process or it will curdle. Transfer to a bowl and season to taste with salt and pepper.

2 For the **Béarnaise Sauce**, pour the vinegar into a small pan and add the shallots, 1 tablespoon of the tarragon, the thyme, and the bay leaf. Bring to a boil and continue to boil until reduced to 1 tablespoon. Strain into a bowl and let cool. Put the egg yolks, cooled vinegar reduction, and water into the blender and process on low speed very briefly. With the motor running, gradually add the melted butter through the hole in the lid. Continue to process until the sauce is thickened. Do not over-process or it will curdle. Transfer to a bowl. Stir in the remaining tarragon and season to taste with salt and pepper.

3 For the **Mousseline Sauce**, put the egg yolks, lemon juice, and water into the blender and process on low speed very briefly to mix. With the motor running, gradually add the melted butter through the hole in the lid. Continue to process until the sauce is thickened. Do not over-process or it will curdle. Transfer to a bowl and season to taste with salt and pepper. Using a rubber spatula, gently fold in the whipped cream.

ASPARAGUS SAUCE

This old-fashioned sauce has a delicate flavor and is an attractive color.
It is delicious with plainly cooked poultry or fish.

Makes about 1 ¼ cups
Preparation time: 15 minutes
Cooking time: 25 minutes

Ingredients

⅔ cup chicken stock	1 lb 9 oz green asparagus
1 bouquet garni, consisting of 3 fresh parsley	3 tablespoons butter
sprigs, 2 fresh thyme sprigs, 1 bay leaf, and a	4 tbsp chopped fresh parsley
small celery stalk tied together	2 tbsp all-purpose flour
2 mushrooms, chopped	1 tbsp superfine sugar
6 scallions, chopped	salt and pepper

1 Put the chicken stock into a pan and add the bouquet garni, mushrooms, and 2 of the scallions. Bring to a boil, then lower the heat, cover, and simmer gently for 20 minutes.

2 Meanwhile, trim off and discard the woody ends of the asparagus stems. Blanch in lightly salted, boiling water for 2 minutes, then drain, and refresh under cold water. Drain well again.

3 Melt 2 tablespoons of the butter in a heavy skillet over medium heat. Add the asparagus, parsley, and remaining scallions and cook, stirring gently, for 5 minutes. Remove from the heat.

4 Using a fork, mash the remaining butter with the flour to a paste to make beurre manié. Remove and discard the bouquet garni from the chicken stock. Stir in the beurre manié in small pieces at a time until they are absorbed and the mixture is thickened. Remove from the heat and let cool slightly.

5 Transfer the asparagus mixture to the blender and add the sugar. Add 4 tablespoons of the chicken stock mixture and season with salt and pepper. Process to a smooth purée, adding chicken stock mixture until you achieve the desired consistency. Stop and scrape down the sides as necessary. Taste and adjust the seasoning, adding more sugar, salt, and pepper as required (the sauce should be quite sweet).

Variation
For a simpler version of this sauce, omit step 1 and don't
bother to add the extra flavors to the chicken stock, but do
thicken it as in step 4. If the final sauce lacks color, you
can add a few drops of green liquid food coloring.

SATAY SAUCE

The mainstay of all barbecues, this sauce is great with kabobs, grilled pork or chicken, and also goes well with salads such as Indonesian gado-gado.

Makes about 1 cup

Preparation time: 10 minutes

Cooking time: 5 minutes

Ingredients

4 scallions, coarsely chopped

1 garlic clove, coarsely chopped

2 tsp chopped fresh ginger root

6 tbsp peanut butter

1 tsp molasses sugar

1 tsp Thai fish sauce

2 tbsp soy sauce

1 tbsp chili or Tabasco sauce

1 tsp lemon juice

salt

coarsely crushed peanuts, to garnish

1 Put all the ingredients, except the crushed peanuts, into the blender. Add 2/3 cup water and process to a purée.

2 Transfer to a pan, season to taste with salt, and heat gently, stirring occasionally. Transfer to a bowl and sprinkle with the crushed peanuts. Serve warm or cold.

Cook's tip
You can use smooth or crunchy peanut butter. However, if you use sweetened peanut butter, omit the sugar. If the sauce is too thick, stir in a little canned coconut milk and reheat gently.

Variation
For a more authentic flavor, substitute tamarind for the lemon juice. Soak 1 teaspoon tamarind pulp in 3 tablespoons warm water, then press through a strainer into a bowl. You could also add 1 chopped lemongrass stalk to the sauce in step 1.

SLIM-LINE SALAD DRESSING

When you're watching your waistline, it's no good serving salads and then smothering them in high-calorie dressings, so here's a good alternative.

 Serves 4

Preparation time: 5 minutes

Cooking time: 0 minutes

Ingredients

Basic Slim-Line Salad Dressing

1 ¼ cups plain
  low-fat yogurt

1 tsp hot mustard

2–3 tbsp lemon juice

4 tsp sunflower oil

salt and pepper

Curry Dressing

1 ¼ cups plain
  low-fat yogurt

2 tsp curry paste

2–3 tbsp red wine vinegar

4 tsp sunflower oil

salt and pepper

Green Dressing

1 ¼ cups plain
  low-fat yogurt

2 tsp Dijon mustard

2–3 tbsp white wine vinegar

4 tsp sunflower oil

2 tbsp coarsely chopped
  fresh parsley

2 tbsp coarsely snipped
  fresh chives

2 tbsp coarsely chopped
  fresh tarragon

1 coarsely chopped scallion

1 tbsp coarsely chopped
  watercress or arugula

salt and pepper

1 To make the **Basic Slim-Line Salad Dressing**, put all the ingredients into the blender and season to taste with salt and pepper. Process on medium speed until thoroughly combined.

2 To make the **Curry Dressing**, put all the ingredients into the blender and season to taste with salt and pepper. Process on medium speed until thoroughly combined.

3 To make the **Green Dressing**, put the yogurt, mustard, vinegar, and oil into the blender and season to taste with salt and pepper. Process on medium speed until thoroughly combined. Add the parsley, chives, tarragon, scallion, and watercress and process for a few seconds to chop finely and blend.

Cook's tip
If the Slim-Line Salad Dressing or the Curry Dressing is thicker than you like, stir in 3–4 tablespoons of skim milk at the end. If you want to dilute the Green Dressing, add the milk and process briefly before adding the herbs.

FRUIT COULIS

You can make a delicious sauce from most soft fruits to
go with ice cream, mousses, and other desserts.

Makes about 1 1/4 cups

Preparation time: 5–10 minutes, plus 1 hour's chilling

Cooking time: 0 minutes

Ingredients

Peach Coulis	Melba Sauce	Tropical Fruit Coulis
1 lb peaches	2 2/3 cups raspberries, fresh or	1 mango
1 tbsp lemon juice	frozen	1 papaya
2 tbsp superfine sugar	1 tbsp lemon juice	3 kiwi fruit
2 tbsp Amaretto liqueur	3 tbsp superfine sugar	2 tbsp superfine sugar
		3 tbsp white rum

1 To make the **Peach Coulis**, using a sharp knife, cut a cross in the base of each peach, then plunge into boiling water for 15–30 seconds. Drain and refresh in ice water. Peel off the skins, halve the peaches, and remove the pits, then slice coarsely. Put the peaches, lemon juice, and sugar into the blender. Process to a smooth purée, scraping down the sides as necessary. Transfer to a bowl and stir in the liqueur. Cover and chill for 1 hour.

2 It is not necessary to thaw frozen raspberries for **Melba Sauce**. Put the fruit, lemon juice, and sugar into the blender. Process to a smooth purée, scraping down the sides as necessary, then rub through a fine nylon strainer into a bowl to remove the seeds. Cover and chill for 1 hour.

3 For the **Tropical Fruit Coulis**, cut the mango lengthwise on either side of the large flat pit. Cut a criss cross pattern in the flesh of the 2 slices without cutting through the skin. Turn inside out so the flesh resembles a porcupine and slice it off the skin. Cut any remaining flesh away from the pit and put it all into the blender. Cut the papaya in half lengthwise and scoop out the seeds with a spoon. Scoop out any fibers. Discard the seeds and fibers. Either cut or scoop the flesh, chop coarsely, and add to the blender. Slice the kiwis and add to the blender with the sugar. Process to a purée, scraping down the sides as necessary, then rub through a fine nylon strainer into a bowl. Stir in the rum. Cover and chill for 1 hour.

Cook's tip
If you are serving these coulis to children, substitute
peach nectar for the Amaretto and orange juice
for the rum.

CUSTARD

Custard is something of a family favorite and this group of recipes includes confectioner's custard for flan fillings and chocolate sauce.

Makes 2 1/2 cups (Custard); 1 1/2 cups (Confectioner's Custard and Easy Chocolate Sauce)

Preparation time: 5 minutes

Cooking time: 5 minutes

Ingredients

Custard	Confectioner's Custard	Easy Chocolate Sauce
1/4 cup cornstarch	1/2 cup sugar	4 oz semisweet chocolate,
2 1/2 cups milk	2 eggs	broken into pieces
1/4 cup sugar	4 tbsp all-purpose flour	2/3 cup light cream
2 tbsp sweet butter	1/2 tsp vanilla extract	generous 1 cup superfine sugar
1 egg	1 1/4 cups milk	1/2 teaspoon rum extract
1/2 tsp vanilla extract	1 tbsp sweet butter	(optional)

1 To make the **Custard**, put the cornstarch into a bowl with 3 tablespoons of the milk. Stir to a paste. Put the remaining milk in a pan and bring just to a boil. Meanwhile, put the sugar, butter, egg, and vanilla extract into the blender and process until smooth. Pour the hot milk into the cornstarch mixture, stirring constantly. Return to the pan and cook over low heat, stirring constantly, for 2 minutes or until thickened With the blender motor running, pour the hot cornstarch mixture into the blender.

2 To make the **Confectioner's Custard**, put the sugar, eggs, flour, vanilla extract, and milk into the blender and process until smooth. Pour into a pan and bring to simmering point, stirring constantly. Cook, stirring, until thick. Remove from the heat and stir in the butter. Set aside to cool before using.

3 To make the **Chocolate Sauce**, put half the chocolate into the blender and process to chop, then add the remainder and process again. Pour the cream into a small pan and bring just to simmering point. Add the cream, sugar, and rum extract, if using, and process until smooth.

Cook's tip
Keep the custard or sauce warm in a bain marie or heatproof bowl set over a pan of gently simmering water. Whisk occasionally.

CHAPTER 3: PURÉES AND DIPS

TARAMASALATA

This popular Greek dip was originally made from smoked gray mullet roe, but this can be difficult to get, so this recipe uses smoked cod's roe.

Serves 6

Preparation time: 15 minutes

Cooking time: 0 minutes

Ingredients

2 slices white bread, crusts removed

5 tbsp milk

8 oz smoked cod's roe

2 garlic cloves, coarsely chopped

2/3 cup olive oil

2 tbsp lemon juice

2 tbsp strained plain yogurt

pepper

black olives, to garnish

1 Tear the bread into pieces and place in a shallow bowl. Add the milk and set aside to soak. Meanwhile, using a sharp knife, scrape the cod's roe away from the outer skin.

2 Tip the bread and milk into the blender and process until smooth. Add the cod's roe and garlic and process again. With the motor running, gradually pour in the olive oil through the hole in the lid. Process until smooth and with the consistency of mayonnaise.

3 Add the lemon juice and yogurt and season with pepper. Process very briefly to mix, then scrape into a bowl. Cover with plastic wrap and chill in the refrigerator until required. Garnish with black olives just before serving.

Cook's tip

Taramasalata is best made with quite a light-tasting olive oil, so don't use one from the Greek mainland, as these tend to be quite aggressive. Italian oils are lighter.

HUMMUS

This popular Middle-Eastern dip, made with garbanzo beans and tahini (sesame seed paste) is also good with salads and lamb chops.

Serves 6

Preparation time: 10 minutes

Cooking time: 0 minutes

Ingredients

1²⁄₃ cups cooked or drained canned
   garbanzo beans

²⁄₃ cup tahini, well stirred

²⁄₃ cup olive oil, plus extra to serve

2 garlic cloves, coarsely chopped

6 tbsp lemon juice

1 tbsp chopped fresh mint

salt and pepper

1 tsp paprika

1 Put the garbanzo beans, tahini, olive oil, and ²⁄₃ cup water into the blender and process briefly.
Add the garlic, lemon juice, and mint and process until smooth.

2 Check the consistency of the hummus and, if it is too thick, add 1 tablespoon water and process again.
Continue adding water, 1 tablespoon at a time, until the right consistency is achieved. Hummus should
have a thick, coating consistency. Season with salt and pepper.

3 Spoon the hummus into a serving dish. Make a shallow hollow in the top and drizzle with
2–3 tablespoons olive oil. Cover with plastic wrap and chill until required. To serve, dust lightly
with paprika.

Cook's tip
*To cook dried garbanzo beans, soak ³⁄₄ cup dried
garbanzos in cold water overnight. Drain, place in a pan,
and add cold water to cover. Bring to a boil, then lower
the heat, and cook for 2–2¹⁄₂ hours until tender. Drain
well and let cool.*

Variation
*Strictly speaking, this dip is called hummus bi tahini.
You can also make plain hummus by omitting the
sesame seed paste if you find the flavor too intense.*

SMOKED TROUT PÂTÉ

The delicate flavor and color of smoked trout makes it the perfect choice when entertaining—and it's not expensive either.

Serves 4

Preparation time: 15 minutes, plus 1 hour's chilling

Cooking time: 0 minutes

Ingredients

4 smoked trout fillets, about 7 oz each

1/2 cup cottage cheese

2/3 cup crème fraîche or sour cream

2 tbsp lemon juice

salt and pepper

lemon twists and fresh chervil

  sprigs, to garnish

rye or brown bread and butter, to serve

1 Skin the fish fillets and flake the flesh. Place the fish in the blender. Add the cottage cheese, crème fraîche, and lemon juice and season with salt and pepper to taste.

2 Process until smooth, scraping down the sides as necessary. Spoon the pâté into 4 ramekins and smooth the surface. Cover with plastic wrap and chill in the refrigerator for at least 1 hour.

3 To serve, uncover the ramekins and garnish each with a small twist of lemon and a sprig of chervil. Serve the pâté with slices of rye or brown bread and butter.

Variation

You could also make this pâté with other hot-smoked fish, such as mackerel or kippers. It would also work well with smoked monkfish, but this is very expensive.

INSTANT PANTRY PÂTÉ

This cheap and cheerful pâté is very popular with children and is a good way to encourage them to eat some healthy oily fish.

 Serves 6

 Preparation time: 10 minutes

 Cooking time: 0 minutes

Ingredients

9 oz canned sardines in oil, drained

1 cup farmer's cheese

2 tbsp tomato ketchup

1 tbsp lemon juice

salt and pepper

lemon slice, to serve (optional)

1 Split open the sardines with a knife and remove and discard the back bones. Scrape off and discard the skin. It doesn't matter if the flesh breaks up.

2 Put the sardines, cheese, ketchup, and lemon juice into the blender and process until smooth. Season to taste with salt and pepper.

3 Spoon into a serving dish, cover with plastic wrap, and keep in the refrigerator until required. Remove from the refrigerator 30 minutes before serving as this pâté tastes best at room temperature. Garnish with a slice of lemon if you like.

Cook's tip
Children will enjoy eating this with raw vegetables such as carrot batons, little celery stalks, whole cherry tomatoes, and cucumber batons. It also goes well with oatcakes.

Variation
You can use virtually any canned, oily fish, such as mackerel or tuna instead of sardines.

CHICKEN LIVER PÂTÉ

This creamy pâté is extremely quick and easy to make and is ideal for serving with Melba toast as a dinner party appetizer.

Serves 6

Preparation time: 15 minutes, plus cooling, and 2 hours' chilling

Cooking time: 5–8 minutes

Ingredients

8 oz chicken livers

2/3 cup butter

2 garlic cloves, coarsely chopped

2 tsp chopped fresh sage leaves

2 tbsp Marsala wine

2/3 cup heavy cream

salt and pepper

To garnish

1/4 cup butter

4–6 fresh sage leaves

1 Trim the chicken livers and chop coarsely. Melt 1/2 cup of the butter in a heavy skillet. Add the chicken livers and cook over medium heat for 5–8 minutes until browned all over but still pink inside. Remove the skillet from the heat.

2 Transfer the chicken livers, in small batches, to the blender and process. Return all the livers to the blender and add the garlic, sage leaves, and remaining butter. Season with salt and pepper.

3 Pour the Marsala into the skillet and stir with a wooden spoon, scraping up any sediment, then add the mixture to the blender. Process until the pâté is smooth and thoroughly mixed. Add the cream and process again to mix. Spoon the pâté into individual pots and let cool completely.

4 Melt the butter for the garnish in a small pan over low heat. Remove the pan from the heat and pour the melted butter over the surface of the cooled pâté. Arrange the sage leaves on top. Let cool, then cover with plastic wrap, and chill for at least 1 hour.

Cook's tip
To make Melba toast, lightly toast both sides of white bread slices until golden. Remove to a board and cut off the crusts. Using a long bread knife, slice horizontally through each slice to make 2 slices. Toast the uncooked sides until golden, then cut into triangles.

Variation
You can substitute either sweet or dry sherry, whichever you prefer, for the Marsala.

GUACAMOLE

Using the blender guarantees that this is a very smooth version of the spicy Mexican dip. It's great with tortilla chips and also goes well with broiled steak.

◎ Serves 6

Preparation time: 10 minutes

Cooking time: 0 minutes

Ingredients

juice of 1 lime	2 tbsp olive oil
3 avocados	1 tbsp sour cream
2 garlic cloves, chopped	salt
3 scallions, chopped	cayenne pepper, to garnish
2 fresh green chilies, seeded and chopped	

1 Put the lime juice into the blender. Halve the avocados and remove the pits. Scoop out the avocado flesh with a spoon straight into the blender.

2 Add the garlic, scallions, chilies, olive oil, and sour cream and season with salt. Process until smooth. Taste and adjust the seasoning with more salt or lime juice.

3 Spoon the guacamole into a serving dish. Dust lightly with cayenne pepper and serve immediately.

Cook's tip
If you are making this in advance, delay adding the garnish. Cover the dish tightly with plastic wrap and keep in the refrigerator for up to 2 hours. Stir, then garnish, and serve. After 2 hours, the dip will begin to discolor.

Variation
For an unusual dip based on guacamole, put 1 tbsp lemon juice, 9 oz chopped cooked beet, 2 chopped garlic cloves, 1/2 cup fresh white bread crumbs, 3 tbsp olive oil, and 2 tbsp creamed horseradish into the blender. Process until smooth and season with salt and pepper.

RED BELL PEPPER DIP

This eye-catching, colorful dip is a good addition to a party buffet table and tastes great with a selection of crisp raw vegetables.

🍽 Serves 6

🥄 Preparation time: 10 minutes, plus cooling

🧤 Cooking time: 10–15 minutes

Ingredients

2 red bell peppers, halved and seeded

2 garlic cloves

1 tbsp olive oil

1 tbsp lemon juice

½ cup fresh white bread crumbs

salt and pepper

1 Place the bell pepper halves and garlic in a pan and add just enough water to cover. Bring to a boil, then lower the heat, cover, and simmer gently for 10–15 minutes until softened and tender. Drain and set aside to cool.

2 Coarsely chop the bell pepper halves and garlic and place in the blender with the olive oil and lemon juice. Process to a smooth purée.

3 Add the bread crumbs and process briefly until just combined. Season to taste with salt and pepper. Transfer to a serving bowl, cover with plastic wrap, and chill in the refrigerator until required.

Cook's tip
Don't forget that the quickest and easiest way to make bread crumbs is in the blender.

Variation
You could also make this dip with orange or yellow bell peppers. Green bell peppers are not really suitable as they are rather acidic.

PEANUT BUTTER

Popular for sandwiches and snacks, peanut butter is also a useful ingredient when baking cookies and, of course, for Satay Sauce (see page 42).

Makes about 8 oz

Preparation time: 5 minutes

cooking time: 0 minutes

Ingredients

Smooth Peanut Butter

2 cups salted peanuts

3 tbsp peanut oil

Crunchy Peanut Butter

2 cups salted peanuts

3 tbsp peanut oil

1 For **Smooth Peanut Butter**, put the peanuts into the blender and process to chop them. With the motor running, gradually add the oil through the hole in the lid. Spoon into a screw-top jar and store in the refrigerator.

2 For **Crunchy Peanut Butter**, put the peanuts into the blender and process to chop coarsely. Remove 8 tablespoons of the chopped nuts and set aside. With the motor running, gradually add the oil to the blender through the hole in the lid. Spoon the mixture into a bowl and stir in the chopped nuts, then transfer to a screw-top jar, and store in the refrigerator.

Variation

Other nut butters are literally made with butter. Blanch 1 cup nuts in boiling water for 1 minute, then drain, and rinse in cold water. Place in the blender with 1 tablespoon cold water and process to a purée. Beat the purée into 1 cup softened sweet butter.

BABA GHANOUSH

This popular Middle-Eastern dip has a wonderfully creamy consistency and is great served simply with warm pita bread.

🍽 Serves 6

🥄 Preparation time: 15 minutes, plus cooling

🍳 Cooking time: 1 hour

Ingredients

2 large eggplant

1 garlic clove, chopped

2 tsp ground cumin

4 tbsp tahini

2 tbsp lemon juice

4 tbsp plain yogurt

2 tbsp chopped fresh cilantro, plus
    extra to garnish

1 Preheat the oven to 425°F. Prick the eggplant skins and place them on a cookie sheet. Bake for 1 hour, or until very soft. Remove from the oven and let cool.

2 Peel off and discard the eggplant skins. Coarsely chop the flesh and place in the blender. Add the garlic, cumin, tahini, lemon juice, yogurt, and cilantro and process until smooth and combined, scraping down the sides as necessary.

3 Transfer to a serving dish, sprinkle with a little cilantro, and serve. If you are cooking ahead, cover the dish tightly with plastic wrap and store in the refrigerator until 30 minutes before serving.

Cook's tip
For a really authentic flavor, grill the eggplant over a barbecue to give them a smoky taste.

CHILI PINEAPPLE DIP

You can make this dip as spicy or as mild as you like—its unusual flavor will certainly be a talking point among your guests.

Serves 6

Preparation time: 10 minutes

Cooking time: 10 minutes

Ingredients

2 tbsp olive oil

2 onions, chopped

8 oz fresh pineapple, chopped

½–1 tsp chili powder

1 tsp ground cinnamon

1 tbsp white wine vinegar

salt

1 Heat the oil in a heavy skillet. Add the onions and pineapple and cook over low heat, stirring occasionally, for 10 minutes, or until golden.

2 Using a slotted spoon, and draining off as much oil as possible, transfer the onion and pineapple mixture to the blender. Add chili powder to taste, the cinnamon, and vinegar and season to taste with salt. Process until smooth.

3 Transfer to a serving dish, cover tightly with plastic wrap, and chill in the refrigerator until required.

Variation
You can also use canned pineapple. Drain well before chopping. Cook the onions for 5 minutes before adding the pineapple to the pan.

CHAPTER 4: SMOOTHIES AND DRINKS

MELON MEDLEY

Both watermelons and cantaloupes are among the most thirst-quenching fruits in the world and are perfect for summer drinks.

 Serves 4

Preparation time: 10 minutes

Cooking time: 0 minutes

Ingredients

Ginger Whizz

1 cantaloupe melon, halved
   and seeded
1 ½-inch piece fresh ginger
   root, chopped
2 tbsp chopped fresh mint
chilled dry ginger or sparkling
   mineral water, to top off

Melon & Mango Tango

1 cantaloupe melon, halved
   and seeded
2½ cups mango juice
2 tbsp fresh orange juice

Wild Watermelon

½ watermelon
1¼ cups vodka

Watermelon Sunset

1 watermelon, halved
6 tbsp fresh ruby grapefruit juice
6 tbsp fresh orange juice
dash of lime juice

1 To make the **Ginger Whizz**, scoop out the melon flesh with a spoon straight into the blender. Add the ginger and mint and process until smooth. Pour into chilled glasses, top off with dry ginger or sparkling mineral water to taste, stir, and serve.

2 To make the **Melon & Mango Tango**, scoop out the melon flesh with a spoon straight into the blender. Add the mango and orange juices and process until smooth. Pour into chilled glasses and serve.

3 To make the **Wild Watermelon**, seed the melon if you were unable to find a seedless one. Scoop the flesh into the blender and process to a purée. Pour into a pitcher and stir in the vodka. Pour into chilled glasses and serve.

4 To make the **Watermelon Sunset**, seed the melon if you were unable to find a seedless one. Scoop the flesh into the blender and add the grapefruit juice, orange juice, and a dash of lime juice. Process until smooth, then pour into chilled glasses, and serve.

Cook's tip
You can add ice cubes to the drinks to cool them, although this will dilute them. It is better to chill the ingredients and glasses first.

FRUIT FANTASY

Fruity drinks provide a great pick-me-up at any time of day and are perfect for giving an energy boost first thing in the morning.

 Serves 4

 Preparation time: 10 minutes

 Cooking time: 0 minutes

Ingredients

Fruit Kefir

1 banana

1 cup strawberries, halved

1 cup peach yogurt

2 tbsp honey

1 cup apple juice, chilled

Breakfast Bar

14 oz canned grapefruit and
   orange segments

4 tbsp lemon juice

3 tbsp lime juice

scant 2 cups orange
   juice, chilled

Perky Pineapple

handful of cracked ice

2 bananas

1 cup pineapple juice, chilled

½ cup lime juice

1 To make the **Fruit Kefir**, peel the banana and slice it directly into the blender. Add the strawberries, yogurt, and honey and process until smooth. With the motor running, pour in the apple juice through the hole in the lid. Pour into chilled glasses and serve.

2 To make the **Breakfast Bar**, tip the canned fruit and the can juices into the blender. Add the lemon, lime, and orange juice and process until smooth. Pour into chilled glasses and serve.

3 To make the **Perky Pineapple**, put the cracked ice into the blender. Peel the bananas and slice directly into the blender. Add the pineapple and lime juice and process until smooth. Pour into chilled glasses and serve.

Cook's tip

If you can't find a can of mixed grapefruit and orange segments, then substitute canned pink grapefruit.

MOCHA SHOCKER

*Coffee and chocolate are two of the most popular flavors
for drinks and they also make a superb combination.*

Serves: 2
Preparation time: 10 minutes
Cooking time: 0 minutes

Ingredients

Mocha Flip-Flop	Mocha Slush	Super Mocha Slush
1¼ cups strong black coffee, chilled	handful of cracked ice	handful of cracked ice
½ cup milk	½ cup coffee syrup	½ cup Kahlúa
2 tbsp chocolate ice cream	¼ cup chocolate syrup	¼ cup crème de cacao
	1 cup chilled milk	1 cup cream
	chocolate curls, to decorate	grated chocolate, to decorate

1 To make the **Mocha Flip-Flop**, put the coffee, milk, and ice cream into the blender. Process for 1 minute, then pour into chilled glasses, and serve.

2 To make the **Mocha Slush**, put the ice into the blender and pour in the coffee syrup, the chocolate syrup, and the milk. Process until slushy. Pour into chilled glasses, decorate with chocolate curls, and serve.

3 To make the **Super Mocha Slush**, put the ice into the blender and pour in the Kahlúa, crème de cacao, and light cream. Process until slushy. Pour into chilled glasses, decorate with grated chocolate, and serve.

Cook's tip
*To crack ice, wrap ice cubes in a clean dish towel, gather
up the corners to make a bag, and bang the ice hard
against a wall several times.*

SODA FOUNTAIN

Fortunately, you don't need a hefty piece of machinery to make your own ice cream sodas and drinks—just a blender.

 Serves 1

Preparation time: 5 minutes

Cooking time: 0 minutes

Ingredients

Simple Soda

1 tbsp vanilla ice cream

2 canned peach halves, drained
  and coarsely chopped

4 tbsp light cream

2/3 cup soda, chilled

Typically Tropical

1 papaya

1 tbsp coconut ice cream

2 tbsp lime juice

2/3 cup soda, chilled

Tutti Frutti

1 tbsp strawberry ice cream

1/2 banana

1/2 pear, peeled, cored,
  and chopped

4 tbsp milk

2/3 cup soda, chilled

1 To make the **Simple Soda**, put the ice cream, peach halves, cream, and soda into the blender. Process for 1–2 minutes, pour into a chilled glass and serve.

2 To make the **Typically Tropical**, halve the papaya lengthwise and scoop out all the seeds (they are very peppery). Scoop out the flesh directly into the blender and add the ice cream, lime juice, and soda. Process for 1–2 minutes, then pour into a chilled glass, and serve.

3 To make the **Tutti Frutti**, put the ice cream into the blender. Peel and slice the banana directly into the blender and add the pear, milk, and soda. Process for 1–2 minutes, pour into a chilled glass, and serve.

BRILLIANT BERRIES

Soft fruits make wonderfully colorful and tasty drinks. This is a great way to encourage your children to eat more fruit.

|O| Serves 4

Preparation time: 5 minutes

Cooking time: 0 minutes

Ingredients

Merry Berry

large handful of crushed ice

4 cups strawberries

1/2 cup grenadine

dry ginger , to top off

Cool Cranberries

3 cups cranberries, thawed if frozen

scant 2 cups cranberry juice, chilled

1 1/4 cups plain yogurt

2–3 tbsp honey

Strawberry Colada

4 cups strawberries

1/2 cup coconut cream

2 1/2 cups pineapple juice, chilled

1 To make the **Merry Berry**, put the crushed ice into the blender. Reserve 4 strawberries for decoration and put the remainder into the blender with the grenadine. Process until smooth, then pour into chilled glasses, and top off with dry ginger. Decorate each glass with a strawberry and serve.

2 To make the **Cool Cranberries**, place the berries and juice in the blender and process until smooth. Add the yogurt and the honey and process again until combined. Taste and add more honey if necessary. Pour into chilled glasses and serve.

3 To make the **Strawberry Colada**, reserve 4 strawberries to decorate. Halve the remainder and place in the blender. Add the coconut cream and pineapple juice and process until smooth, then pour into chilled glasses, decorate with the reserved strawberries, and serve.

Variation
You can substitute your favorite berries in any of these recipes—raspberries for strawberries (remember that they have seeds) or blackberries for cranberries, for example.

GOING NUTS

Nuts are little powerhouses of energy, so these drinks and smoothies are quick ways to restore get-up-and-go whenever you're beginning to flag.

Serves 2

Preparation time: 10 minutes

Cooking time: 30–60 seconds (Almond Milk and Double A)

Ingredients

Almond Milk

¼ cup blanched almonds

1¼ cups milk, chilled

½ cup plain yogurt

2 tbsp superfine sugar

Choconut Special

2 bananas

4 tbsp smooth peanut butter

2 scoops chocolate ice cream

1¼ cups chilled milk

chopped peanuts, to decorate

Double A

¼ cup blanched almonds

8 oz canned apricot halves in natural juice

⅔ cup apricot yogurt

¼ tsp ground cloves

1 To make the **Almond Milk**, dry-fry the almonds in a heavy skillet, tossing and turning frequently, for 30–60 seconds until golden. Remove from the heat and let cool, then place in the blender, and process until finely chopped. Add the milk, yogurt, and sugar and process until smooth. Pour into chilled glasses and serve.

2 To make the **Choconut Special**, peel and slice the banana directly into the blender. Add the peanut butter, ice cream, and milk and process until combined. Pour into chilled glasses, decorate with a sprinkling of chopped peanuts, and serve with a straw.

3 To make the **Double A**, dry-fry the almonds in a heavy skillet, tossing and turning frequently, for 30–60 seconds until golden. Remove from the heat and let cool, then place in the blender, and process until finely chopped. Drain the apricots, reserving half the can juice. Coarsely chop the apricots and add to the blender with the reserved juice. Process briefly, add the yogurt and cloves, and process again until smooth. Pour into chilled glasses and serve.

Cook's tip
Always check nuts for freshness before using—while they are a very useful pantry ingredient, they can go off if kept for too long.

FIVE A DAY

People often overlook vegetables as ingredients for drinks and smoothies, but lots of them are really fabulous.

Serves 2
Preparation time: 10 minutes
Cooking time: 0 minutes

Ingredients

24 Carrot
handful of cracked ice
2 carrots, coarsely chopped
4 oz canned pineapple pieces
   in juice, drained
¾ cup pineapple juice, chilled
cucumber slices, to decorate

In the Pink

1 blood orange
2-inch piece of cucumber,
   peeled and cut into chunks
1¼ cups tomato juice,
   chilled
dash of Worcestershire sauce
salt
cucumber slices, to decorate

On the Beet

6 oz cooked beet, chopped
½ cup orange juice, chilled
5 tbsp plain yogurt, chilled
⅔ cup still mineral water,
   chilled
salt
orange slices, to decorate

1 To make the **24 Carrot**, put the ice into the blender, add the carrots, pineapple pieces, and pineapple juice, and process until slushy. Pour into chilled glasses, decorate with cucumber slices, and serve with straws.

2 To make the **In the Pink**, peel the orange, removing all traces of white pith. Holding it over a plate to catch the juice, cut out the segments from the membranes. Squeeze the membranes over the plate to extract any juice. Place the segments and the juice in the blender. Add the cucumber and tomato juice and season to taste with Worcestershire sauce and salt. Process at high speed, then strain into chilled glasses and serve, decorated with cucumber slices.

3 To make the **On the Beet**, put the beet, orange juice, yogurt, and water into the blender and season to taste with salt. Process until smooth, then pour into chilled glasses, and serve, decorated with orange slices.

Cook's tip
Cooked beet is well known for staining hands and fingers—you could wear protective gloves while handling it to avoid this.

CHAPTER 5: DESSERTS

EASY ORANGE CHEESECAKE

 *Everyone's favorite, cheesecake is a melt-in-your-mouth dessert
or a special treat served with morning coffee.*

🍽 Serves 6

🥣 Preparation time: 25 minutes, plus 2 hours' chilling

🧤 Cooking time: 5 minutes

Ingredients

4 oz graham crackers

¼ cup butter, plus extra for greasing

1 cup farmer's cheese cheese

⅔ cup plain yogurt

½ packet orange jelly (3½–4 oz),
   torn into cubes

1 tbsp sugar

grated rind and juice of 1 orange

7 oz canned mandarin
   orange segments, drained

1 Break up the graham crackers and process in batches in the blender to make crumbs. Melt the butter in a small pan over low heat. Remove the pan from the heat and stir in the cracker crumbs. Lightly grease an 8-inch loose-based pie pan, then press the buttery crumbs into it. Place in the refrigerator to chill until the crust has set.

2 Meanwhile, place the farmer's cheese and yogurt in the clean blender and process to combine.

3 Heat 3–4 tablespoons water in a small pan, then remove from the heat, and add the jelly. Stir until dissolved, then stir in the sugar and the orange rind and juice. Add the mixture to the blender and process until smooth. Pour the filling into the cracker crumb case and chill in the refrigerator for 2 hours, or until set.

4 Carefully remove the cheesecake from the pan and place on a serving plate. Arrange the mandarin segments around the edge of the cheesecake and serve.

Variation
*This cheesecake also tastes wonderful and looks
lovely decorated with fresh raspberries.*

CHOCOLATE ICE CREAM

*Homemade ice cream is a real treat with its rich texture and delicious
flavors, and chocolate has to be the number one flavor.*

🍽 Serves 4

🥣 Preparation time: 30 minutes, plus cooling and freezing

🧤 Cooking time: 15–20 minutes

Ingredients

1 vanilla bean

3¾ cups milk

4 oz semisweet chocolate, broken into pieces

4 egg yolks

generous ½ cup superfine sugar

1¼ cups heavy cream

salt

1 Slit the vanilla bean lengthwise and place in a pan with the milk. Bring just to simmering point, then
remove from the heat, and set aside. Place the chocolate in a heatproof bowl and set over a pan of
barely simmering water, stirring occasionally, until melted. Do not let the base of the bowl touch the surface
of the water. When the chocolate has melted, remove from the heat, and set aside to cool completely.

2 Remove the vanilla bean and stir the chocolate into the milk. Put the egg yolks and sugar into the
blender, pour in the chocolate milk, and add a pinch of salt. Process until thoroughly mixed. Pour the
mixture into a heatproof bowl set over a pan of barely simmering water and cook, stirring constantly, until
the custard has thickened and will coat the back of a spoon. Remove from the heat and let cool.

3 Whisk the cream until softly peaking, then fold it into the cooled chocolate custard. Pour the custard into
a freezerproof container, cover, and place in the freezer for 1 hour, or until ice crystals have formed
around the edges. Scoop the ice cream into the blender and process until smooth. Return to the container
and place the container in the freezer for 1 hour.

4 Process the ice cream in the blender again, then return to the freezer. Repeat this process once more,
then freeze until firm. Transfer the container to the refrigerator 15 minutes before serving to let the ice
cream soften slightly.

Cook's tip
*If you have a hand-held blender you can use this to beat
the semi-frozen ice cream without removing it from the
freezerproof container.*

Variation
*To make coffee ice cream, substitute 2 tablespoons instant
coffee powder for the vanilla bean, stirring until they have
dissolved. Omit the chocolate. Alternatively, don't omit the
chocolate and make mocha ice cream.*

PEACH FOOL

This family favorite is easy to make. Although fools are traditionally made with "sour" fruit, such as gooseberries and rhubarb, peaches are scrumptious.

🍽 Serves 4

🥣 Preparation time: 10 minutes, plus 2 hours' chilling

🧤 Cooking time: 0 minutes

Ingredients

8 oz peaches

1 quantity Confectioner's Custard (see page 48)

²/₃ cup heavy cream

amaretti, to serve

1 Using a sharp knife, cut a cross in the base of each peach, then plunge into boiling water for 15–30 seconds. Drain and refresh in ice water. Peel off the skins, halve the peaches, and remove the pits, then slice coarsely.

2 Put the peaches into the blender and process to a smooth purée. Mix the purée into the confectioner's custard until thoroughly combined.

3 Whisk the cream until stiff, then fold it into the custard mixture in 2 batches. Divide among serving dishes or glasses and chill in the refrigerator for at least 2 hours. Serve with amaretti.

Variation
For rhubarb fool, chop 9 oz rhubarb into chunks and place in a pan with 2 tablespoons superfine sugar and 1 tablespoon water. Cover and simmer gently for 10–15 minutes, until softened. Drain and process to a purée and combine with the confectioner's custard.

STRAWBERRY ICE

A simple fruit-flavored "water" ice is one of the most refreshing desserts imaginable at the end of an al fresco lunch on a hot summer's day.

Serves 4

Preparation time: 15 minutes, plus freezing

Cooking time: 0 minutes

Ingredients

4 1/2 cups strawberries, hulled

1/2 cup superfine sugar

1/2 cup orange juice

1 tbsp lemon juice

1 Place the strawberries, sugar, orange juice, and lemon juice in the blender and process until smooth and the sugar has dissolved completely. Taste and add more sugar and/or lemon juice.

2 Pour the mixture into a freezerproof container, cover, and place in the freezer for 1 hour, or until ice crystals have formed around the edges. Scoop the ice into the blender and process until smooth. Return to the container and return the container to the freezer for 1 hour.

3 Process the ice in the blender again, then return to the freezer. Repeat this process once more, then freeze until firm. Transfer the container to the refrigerator 10 minutes before serving to let the ice soften slightly.

Variation

Virtually all soft fruits make delicious ices, so try substituting the same quantity of raspberries or loganberries for the strawberries. Push the purée through a nylon strainer before freezing to remove the seeds.

MELTING MANGO DESSERT

*Luscious mango and spicy ginger is a combination made
in heaven and the perfect way to end any meal.*

Serves 6

Preparation time: 15 minutes, plus 1 hour's chilling

Cooking time: 0 minutes

Ingredients

3 mangoes

3 pieces of preserved ginger in syrup

3 tbsp ginger syrup from the jar

5 tbsp crème fraîche or sour cream

3 egg whites

chopped almonds or pistachios, to decorate

1 Cut the mangoes lengthwise on either side of the large flat pit. Cut a criss-cross pattern in the flesh of the 2 slices without cutting through the skin. Turn inside out so the flesh resembles a porcupine and slice it off the skin. Cut any remaining flesh away from the pit and put it all into the blender

2 Add the preserved ginger, ginger syrup, and crème fraîche and process until smooth. Scrape the purée into a large bowl.

3 Whisk the egg whites in a separate, grease-free bowl until they form soft peaks. Gently fold the egg whites into the mango purée with a rubber spatula. Divide the mixture among serving dishes, cover, and chill in the refrigerator for at least 1 hour. Sprinkle with the chopped nuts before serving.

Cook's tip
Preserved ginger in jars is widely available from supermarkets. It consists of young ginger shoots that have been cooked and preserved in a sugar syrup.

Variation
Substitute 3–4 large ripe bananas for the mangoes. Peel, then slice them directly into the blender.

KIWI SHERBET

Sherbets are a little more substantial than water ice but not so rich as ice cream.
They look great when made with colorful fruits such as kiwi.

○ Serves 6
○ Preparation time: 15 minutes, plus cooling and freezing
○ Cooking time: 5–8 minutes

Ingredients
1 lb 9 oz kiwi fruit
4 tbsp orange juice
$\frac{3}{4}$ cup superfine sugar
strip of thinly pared lemon rind

1 To peel a kiwi, cut a thin slice off both ends, then stand it upright on a cutting board, and slice off the remainder of the skin vertically in strips. Try not to remove too much of the flesh. Peel all the kiwis and cut into fourths. Place them in the blender with the orange juice and process to a purée.

2 Put the sugar and lemon rind in a heavy pan and pour in $\frac{3}{4}$ cup water. Bring to a boil, stirring until the sugar has dissolved, then remove the pan from the heat, and let cool.

3 Remove and discard the lemon rind from the sugar syrup. Stir in the kiwi fruit purée and mix well. Pour the mixture into a freezerproof container, cover, and place in the freezer for 1 hour until ice crystals have formed around the edges. Scoop the sherbet into the blender and process until smooth. Return to the container and replace the container in the freezer for 1 hour.

4 Process the sherbet in the blender again, then return to the freezer. Repeat this process once more, then freeze until firm. Transfer the container to the refrigerator 10 minutes before serving to let the sherbet soften slightly.

Variation
Tropical fruits make colorful sherbets. You could substitute
1 large mango, pitted, peeled, and chopped, for the kiwi
fruit, or 1 lb 9 oz papaya, peeled, seeded, and chopped,
for the kiwis and lime rind and juice for the lemon rind and
orange juice.

ORANGE COEURS À LA CRÈME

These little heart-shaped molds are perfect for Valentine's Day or any time that you're feeling romantic.

Serves 4

Preparation time: 10 minutes, plus 6 hours' chilling

Cooking time: 0 minutes

1 cup ricotta cheese
1 cup mascarpone cheese
¼ cup superfine sugar
grated rind and juice of ½ large orange
Peach Coulis (see page 47), to serve

1 Put the ricotta cheese into a blender and process briefly until smooth. Add the mascarpone, sugar, orange rind, and juice and process until combined.

2 Line 4 coeur à la crème molds with cheesecloth, then spoon the mixture into them. Smooth the surface and place the molds on a flat plate or tray to catch any liquid that drains during setting. Place in the refrigerator and chill for 6 hours or until set.

3 To serve, turn the molds out onto individual plates and surround with a pool of peach coulis.

Cook's tip
If you don't have any coeur à la crème molds, spoon all the mixture into a cheesecloth-lined strainer and set it over a bowl in the refrigerator for 6 hours. To serve, spoon the mixture into lightly greased ramekins, then turn out.

Variation
You can substitute farmer's cheese for the mascarpone and the rind and juice of 1 lemon for the orange rind and juice, if you like.

CRÊPES

These can be as simple or elaborate as you like. Children love them with syrup,

but you can also fill them with cream and fruit or even flambé them in liqueur.

🍽 Serves 4–6

🥣 Preparation time: 10 minutes, plus 15–30 minutes' standing

🧤 Cooking time: 12–15 minutes

Ingredients

2 eggs

scant 2 cups milk

1 ½ cups all-purpose flour, sifted

2 tsp superfine sugar, plus extra for sprinkling

2 tbsp butter, melted

lemon wedges, to serve

1 Put the eggs and milk into the blender and process briefly to combine. With the motor running, gradually add the flour and sugar through the hole in the lid. Process until just combined and free of any lumps, but be careful not to overmix.

2 Pour the batter into a pitcher, cover, and let stand for 15–30 minutes to let the starch grains soften and expand.

3 Heat a crêpe pan over medium heat until it is very hot. Brush with melted butter. Stir the batter and pour 3–4 tablespoons into the pan. Tilt and rotate the pan to spread the batter evenly. Cook for 30–40 seconds until the crêpe is set, the underside is lightly browned, and the top has small holes in it. Shake the pan to loosen, then flip the crêpe over with a spatula or toss, if you prefer. Cook the second side for 30 seconds.

4 Slide the crêpe onto a warm plate and keep warm while you cook the remainder, brushing the pan with more melted butter as required. Stack the crêpes interleaved with waxed paper until you are ready to serve them.

5 To serve, roll or fold the crêpes and place on warm plates. Sprinkle with sugar and serve with lemon wedges for squeezing.

Cook's tip
To test whether the crêpe pan is hot enough, sprinkle a couple of drops of water on the surface. If they sizzle immediately, the pan is ready to use.

Variation
For savory crêpes, simply omit the sugar from the batter. They can be filled with cooked spinach and ricotta cheese or ham and mushrooms and served with Cheese Sauce (see page 36).

INDEX